Copyright Text: Helen Hoyte

ISBN number: 978-0-9559320-2-1

Publisher: Nick Williams

Printer: Broadland Digital Ltd.

Front Cover:

Norwich Shawl 1840s. Towler & Campin. The dye known as Norwich Red is the ground colour.

Back Cover: Norwich Reversable Shawl 1860s probably made by C. & F. Bolingbroke and Jones

The story

of the

NORWICH SHAWL

Helen Hoyte

Helen Hoyte

ACKNOWLEDGEMENTS

My grateful thanks to

the late Pamela Clabburn for her inspiration and for her years of research which she shared so generously,

to Vanessa Trevellyn for allowing the use of images in the collection of the Norfolk Museums and Archaeology Service and for her encouragement to write this book,

to Thelma Morris for preparing the book for publication

and to Vivienne Weeks for her help with photography.

PERMISSION TO USE THE FOLLOWING IMAGES

Interior of Parisian drapery store c1860: Oxford History of Fashion, Christopher Breward

Portraits of Abel and Elizabeth Towler: Mr. William Gowing

Portrait of Harriet Ann Dickenson, the forebear of Mrs. Diana Cooke, published in The Story of Arthur Evans by Joan Evans, 1943: Mrs. Diana Cooke

Models wearing shawls from the event staged by the Costume and Textile Association: The Costume and Textile Association.

Dyeing in medieval times: Waterfront *Excavation at Whitefriars, Norwich 1979, Report No. 17.* East Anglian Archaeology (Ayers and Murphy)

Scenes from the 1851 Great Exhibition: every effort has been made to trace the copyright holder of this image but without success.

This book is dedicated to the memory of the late Pamela Clabburn who, during her time as Curator of the Strangers Hall Museum, first brought to public attention the wealth of beauty contained in the late 18th century and 19th century Norwich Shawls.

INTRODUCTION

When I inherited a fine old Edinburgh shawl it sparked an interest and a desire to see the collection of Norwich shawls, then kept at Strangers Hall Museum.

Having been a textile designer, I was immediately captivated by the beauty of the designs and as I researched the shawls, I became more amazed at the skill and craftsmanship of the old Norwich weavers and printers. Added to the shawls fascination, was the realisation that fashionable shawl-wearing had been for many decades of important social significance. My interest has since become my passion!

This book is not intended for textile specialists. It is for the general public, in the hope that the story of the magnificent shawls will be of interest and awaken a pride in this branch of the great bygone Norwich Textile Industry.

My grateful thanks to the Harry Watson Bursary for providing financial support, without which this book would not have been possible.

Proceeds from the sale of this book will go to The Costume and Textile Association for Norfolk Museums.

CONTENTS

Nobleman wears shawls
for turban, sash and
shawl manta.
After the painting
'The Indian' by
Anne Louis Girodel-Trioson
1807.

The radical change in
costume at the end of
the 18th century brought
shawls into fashion.

Left: Court Dress 1760

Right: c1810

THE
STORY
BEGINS

Since ancient times shawls, stoles and scarves besides their usefulness, have often been invested with social and religious significance in many different cultures. This story begins with the rising awareness of far Eastern shawls in the 18th century and how they became part of European society. Especially those from Kashmir, where for centuries Royal princes and noblemen had proclaimed their status and importance by wearing their country's magnificent shawls. The word 'shawl' comes from *shâl*, a Persian word which was adopted into Urdu and other Indian languages. In the British lexicon 'shawl' came to mean an upmarket textile accessory, a meaning which was to last for nearly a hundred years.

Traditionally patterned in bright colours and in different sizes and styles, Kashmiri princes could wear two or more expensive shawls at a time, not only over the shoulders, but round the waist and arranged as head turbans. These fine textiles were intended for masculine wear; by the early 18th century British men engaged in Indian trade and politics were choosing to wear shawls and some had their portraits painted, posing in Indian princely styles. In Europe at the end of the 18th century, as the fashion began to take a hold on European society, patterned shawls changed from masculine wear to exclusive feminine costume. Shawls bestowed the same social status enjoyed by Indian princes on European wearers and shawl-wearing seems to have kept the fashionable world in its grip for many decades.

During the 18th century as trade between the two continents developed Indian artefacts, including textiles, fascinated Europeans. Early imports of Indian printed cottons to Britain posed a serious threat to the home textile industry and ladies who wore them risked having their gowns ripped off their backs by hostile workers. East India Company ships' officers were known to bring back fabrics including shawls, to sell and as presents for their families. Ladies who lived in India, brought shawls when they returned home. The writer Laurence Sterne commented that his friend Eliza, when she returned from Bombay in 1765 with several shawls, appeared not to understand that they were unsuitable for female wear. It was not until the end of the century that Europe's fashionable world began to look on shawls as anything but exotic curiosities or masculine accessories.

The stylised patterns and bright colours of Indian shawls were considered too alien and unacceptable to wear with the contemporary European costume of formal gowns in delicately coloured, naturalistic floral patterned silk brocades and damasks. Near the end of the century, the effects of the French Revolution and its dramatic impact on society radically changed the fashionable world. It was no longer acceptable – indeed it could be dangerous – to wear luxurious silks and satins and these were rejected (but only for a few years) in favour of scanty gowns made of flimsy cottons. Immediately, the covering of a large, warm shawl became vital.

Large, soft, light in weight and colourful, Kashmiri shawls became highly desirable and very quickly became the accessory to accompany the thin dresses favoured by wealthy Europeans in the highest society. Amazing archaeological discoveries in Pompei and Herculaneum awakened society's interest in the classical world, and influenced the lifestyle of high society. They also promoted costume ideas modelled on Greek and Roman statues and the lovely draping qualities of cashmere shawls enhanced the fashionable statuesque 'look'.

Many early 19th century portraits depict the growing craze for wearing shawls. Those from Kashmir were prohibitively expensive to all but the very rich and wearing a *'cashmire'* was an indication of the wearer's wealth and status. The finest Kashmiri shawls took the cloth-makers two to three years to complete and the highest quality shawls cost the equivalent of a small European house. Superb textiles in texture and design, they were works of art and the 'must have' for every aspiring lady.

The great Kashmiri shawls were made from the wool of the mountain goat, *Capra Hircus* which lived in the icy conditions of the high Himalayan mountains. In spring, when the goats shed their heavy coats, the very fine under-hair which grew beneath the thick outer fleece was laboriously collected from the high pastures by labourers. It was cleaned and washed, then rigorously combed to collect the longest fibres which were spun to an even and fine thread, ready for dyeing. The time-consuming tapestry method of weaving was used, similar to European wall tapestries. A warp was prepared on a horizontal loom and a series of small bobbins were wound with wool or silk to weave sections of the design into the warp. Seated at the loom, two or three weavers usually worked together; instruction was given to them by the 'colour caller', who read out sequences of numbers from the design plan, prepared by the 'pattern master'. Held in a twill weave, these threads slowly interlocked into the warps to create the coloured pattern. When weaving was finished, any flaws, knots and mistakes were meticulously repaired. It was then taken to the wash-house to be soaked in water and lightly trampled with bare feet, after which the shawl was stretched out in the shade to dry slowly. Finally, finished fringes were added and two shawls were often sewn together back to back, to hide the short ends of yarn on the back of each shawl.

At the end of the 18th century as the craze for wearing shawls spread like wildfire, European textile manufacturers grasped the opportunity to make shawls, producing copies of Indian shawls at cheaper prices than those from Kashmir. As trade expanded, textile manufacturing centres in Britain and France competed fiercely to make shawls for the wealthy middle-classes, whose envy of the Kashmiri shawls had been fostered by their awe and respect for the aristocracy.

The challenge for the European manufacturers was to simulate the soft, light quality of cashmere wool. Early experiments involving the importation of Himalayan goats to warmer climates were not successful. Many wools were too heavy or coarse and it was here in Norwich with its long tradition of cloth making, that one solution was

Himalayan goat

CAPRA HIRCUS

Early European shawl in imitation of Indian shawls

Portrait of Mrs. John Crome (1813-14)
by Michael Sharpe

She wears an early long shawl (sometimes
called a scarf) with patterns on the ends
and narrow borders.

Model is displaying a long shawl c1830s:
cream centre with deep galleries of
pines with narrow borders.

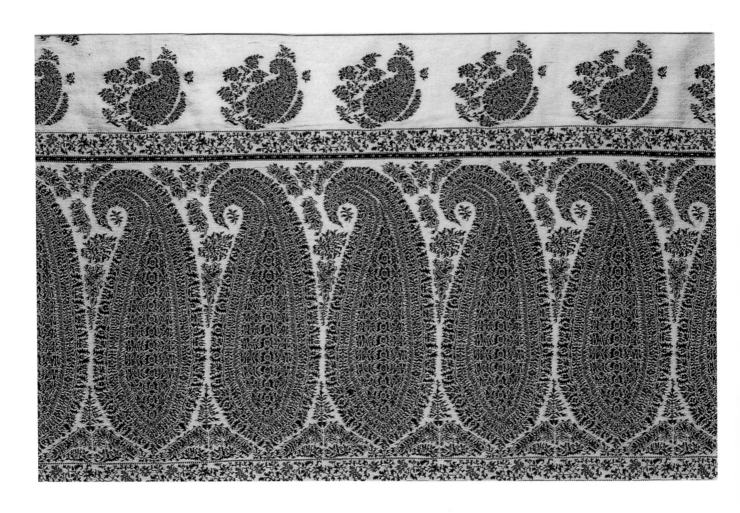

1845 cream shawl with deep galleries and closely filled pines: probably Norwich.
(shawls with similar designs were being made in Paisley)

found. In the 18th century a fabric, made with a silk warp and worsted weft and known as a *half-silk*, had brought great prosperity to the city. This combination of yarns of suitable thickness made a soft, light and warm cloth, and it was quickly seen as ideal for the manufacture of shawls.

Some Norwich worsted manufacturers who had survived the difficulties experienced by the textile industry in the late 1780s welcomed the new shawl-wearing fashion. They soon copied the Indian shawl designs, not by the lengthy method of tapestry weaving, but by using their foot operated shaft handlooms to weave the traditional plain *half-silk* fabric, using embroiderers to darn the coloured pattern motifs into the cloth. At the end of the 18th century, Norwich manufacturers were selling bed-furnishings decorated with embroidered designs and this seems to have been the first shawl makers' method for copying Indian designs onto shawls. In the 1790s there are several references to simulating weaving by embroidery, and in a letter written in 1800, a Lady Jermyn recalls a visit she had made to a house in Magdalen Street in Norwich, where she saw four girls sitting round a table darning the design into the borders of a shawl.

An early attempt by a Norwich manufacturer in shawl patterning in 1785 is recorded. Edward Barrow, advertised

'...a scarf in imitation of the Indian...it proved too dear to sell and manufacture was withdrawn'

Perhaps too early for the fashion to have taken hold in the provinces.

By the end of the century, shawl production in the city was rapidly increasing. Shawls now had simple patterns set into the fabric by the loom and a contemporary account states

'The present looms....producing flowers are as a result of the shuttle passing through only and not entirely across. This is time consuming and a weaver can only weave an inch a day'.

Possibly an indication of the early method known as 'finger-spotting'; women working on each side of the weaver and between each shot of the shuttle, deftly inserting short ends of yarn into the web.

This practice was labour intensive and, always looking to reduce costs, manufacturers were soon patterning the weave on the draw-loom. To create the design, the weaver worked with a draw-boy, who to his instruction, pulled a system of cords attached to the loom. The cords lifted the warp yarns in sequence and the weaver's shuttles, carrying continuous weft threads, stretched from selvage to selvage. As they worked, the patterned cloth was face down on the loom and long floats of yarn built up across the back of the fabric. When weaving was finished, these floats were cropped off, first by hand and later by machine. Cropped yarn, known as shoddy could be re-spun if of good quality, otherwise used for household stuffings.

Shawls woven by this method were known as *fillover* shawls, and by 1815 Norwich weavers were developing some of the most beautiful of the European shawls on the market. An indication of the huge demand can be seen in the account books in the Bridewell Museum, Norwich. Receipts confirm that by the end of the 18th century and at the beginning of the 19th century, shawl production in the City was enormous. Increasingly, businesses were describing themselves as 'Shawl-makers', but it would seem that with too many climbing on the band-wagon, there was a serious threat to prices and a lowering of quality. Sadly, few records remain of the actual manufacturing practices and many of the terms they used to describe the types and styles of shawls are long forgotten and now lost to us.

To own a fine shawl became the aspiration of 19th century society. The status enjoyed by the old Princes of India continued; a lady's shawl would also show her sense of style and the gift of a shawl could express sentiment for very special occasions. These influences were to continue for many decades.

Turnover shawls were fashionable in the early 19th century: square fabric centres in plain colours had borders sewn on, with two of the borders reversed to make the correct V shape at the back.

Below: c1832 crosses in the design appear to show links with the church (possibly a gift to celebrate the marriage of a clergyman to a lady in the family) and in the border a small motif could be a Saracen's cap, a feature of the Walpole Coat of Arms.

1840s.

1850s

19th CENTURY NORWICH SHAWLS

1860s.

1870s

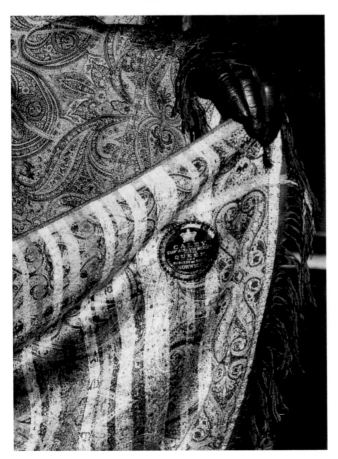

1815

1830

19th Century Costume

1840

1870

FASHION AND THE 19TH CENTURY LADY

The fascination of being 'in fashion' has occupied the hearts and minds of men and women for centuries. 'Clothes', as James Laver the eminent costume historian said, 'are the furniture of the mind made visible, the very mirror of an epoch's soul'. It had always been the prerogative of the aristocracy to be the leaders of fashion, but the industrial revolution in the 19th century with its rising middle classes and increasing affluence, saw new fashionable styles spread to a wider society.

Over the early centuries, changes in costume were introduced by the leaders of fashion in the Royal courts. Wearing stylish costume gave status to top people and in an attempt to preserve it, sumptuary laws were passed, but wealthy social climbers tended to get round them. (Sumptuary laws were passed during the 13th and 17th centuries to protect home industry from costly foreign imports and to maintain a class structure which permitted only persons of rank to wear certain garments, fabrics and decorations.) The early Church had influential views on women's costume and continued to be outspoken in matters of modesty and decorum. In the 17th and 18th centuries the great wealth and privilege enjoyed by the few, saw wild excesses of costume among the leaders of fashion – until the menace of the revolution in France curtailed the affluence, which had sustained such extravagance. Towards the end of the 19th century, as the old order of society was changing again, a growing interest in sport was to have a strong influence on fashionable dress. Into the 20th century and, although Paris remained the centre of fashion for the wealthy, a developing public media of cinema and television, featured and promoted film stars and celebrities who became the style-setters. By the end of the century, fashion ideas were international.

Today, with the enormous mass production of imported clothes, never before has such a wide choice of cheap outfits been so accessible to the general public. Clothes now are mostly functional, comfortable, easy to launder and often would appear to reflect the ethos of our more egalitarian society. Younger generations dress in their own generic styles which reflect their youth and interests, but mostly people wear what they feel is appropriate for them and by the clothes they chose, make statements about their own lifestyles. There is no longer a centre point from which contemporary fashion is dictated for all and such diversity may indeed be an indication of 'the furniture of their minds and an epoch's soul'.

It comes, perhaps as a surprise to realise that for the 19th century lady who wished to be at the top of society, it was important to comply with one of the fashionable demands of her time, that she owned and wore as good a shawl as she could afford and that to Victorian society, shawls had a deeper meaning than just as accessories to her costume.

Despite the Terror of the French Revolution, Paris continued to be the arbiter of fashion. The radical change from formal gowns to thin cotton dresses, cut in a *dishabille* style, was started by the leaders of fashion in Napoleon's Court and spread quickly to Britain and the rest of Europe. Women were soon so scantily dressed, that older generations were deeply shocked. With this dramatic change to thin cotton gowns, a warm and enveloping Indian cashmere shawl became the choice and 'must-have' of the rich aspiring fashionista. As we have seen, European manufacturers were quick to meet the demands of the *nouveau riche* and by undercutting Indian prices, marketed quality copies of the desirable cashmere shawls, but it was to be some time before European shawls were able to supplant the lure of the genuine article.

At first, shawls were long in size, colourful, warm and lightweight coverings for the flimsy gowns of the late 18th century, but gradually in 19th century society, shawl-wearing changed its purpose and became an emblem of femininity and respectability. Not only was it a necessity for warmth, but a good shawl enhanced the wearer's character as well as her status in society.

Imported shawls were expensive. Ranging in quality, the finest Indian cashmere shawls could cost up to 200 guineas, which put the highest quality shawls beyond the reach of all but the very wealthy. As the fashion for shawl wearing began to spread, the social significance of owning an *Indienne Cachmire* became generally accepted and this was to continue into the 19th century. The awe and respect these expensive shawls invited, seems to have imposed a power which transformed the wearers. There are references in contemporary literature to high quality shawls being revered and treasured. It is clear too, that those who owned a shawl created a longing in those of less affluent means. Jane Carlyle commented in a letter in 1830

> *'I am very vain of my beautiful little shawl; so vain that*
> *I rode to Templand with it above my habit'.*

Charlotte Bronte was aware of their influence, in her novel *'Villette'*, written in 1853

> *'.....the spell by which she struck a certain awe through the household, quelling the*
> *otherwise scornfully disposed teachers and servants, so long as her broad*
> *shoulders wore the folds of that majestic drapery.....'un veritable Cachmire'.*

Mrs. Gaskell in her novel 'North and South' in 1855, captures the physical and psychological pleasure as she describes the effect on Margaret when she tries on her aunt's shawls,

Interior of Parisian Drapery Store c1860

Norwich draper's receipt for customer's payment in 1845
for a Fillover Norwich Shawl £7.

'......in the mirror like a princess, she touched the shawls gently as they hung around her,and took pleasure in their soft feel, their gentle colours, liking to be dressed in such splendour'

The ownership of a good shawl could mark a lady's position in society and her choice of fabric and design confirmed her impeccable taste. The style with which a lady wore her shawl was also important. Early in the 19th century, classes were held to instruct ladies in the various ways of draping and displaying their shawls to advantage, their deportment too. Ladies' journals which reported on styles and colours favoured by the Royal family and the Court, were influential and eagerly read. One journal stated

'A lady is known by her taste in her choice of shawl and how she wears it.'

In 1839 the Commissioners in their Report on the Condition of the Hand Loom Weavers observed:

'Ladies of property will not buy a shawl of which there are many designs.'

At the end of the 18th and the early 19th centuries, long shawls with deep galleries of designs at each end and narrow side borders of Indian motifs and colourings were popular. The delightful *turnover* style of shawl became fashionable in the 1820s and 1830s. By the 1840s when skirts had increased in size, larger square shawls with heavier silk or wool fringing came into fashion. In the 1850s to suit full skirts supported by the crinoline, shawls became long again and when the size of the skirt reached its optimum width, huge, pure silk shawls, woven on Jacquard looms could measure nearly four metres in length. It was in the mid 1850s that there was a change in styles of colour; synthetic dyes were replacing those made from natural materials and colours tended to become somewhat harsher.

Before shawls were sold in drapery shops, a lady would go to the manufacturer's warehouse to buy her shawl. There she could chose from a stock of plain cloths the coloured centre she preferred, a woven design border was chosen to go round it, together with the fringe and the shawl was assembled by a skilful needlewoman. Later, shawl emporiums were established in the major high streets where shawls from many centres were displayed.

Small local drapers could obtain shawls directly from the manufacturers and in 1843, a receipt from a draper in Market Street, Norwich, to a customer with a large house in Bracondale, Norwich, itemises

'A Norwich Fillover Shawl at £7'

There were also itinerant peddlers, who carried their wares including shawls, to country houses. Shawl emporiums and shops became the accepted middlemen between the manufacturer (who were often retailers too) and the customer.

British shawls made of silk and wool, could range from £2 to 20 guineas. Cheaper wools were coarse to touch and shawls with a loose weave would be sold at lower prices at around 27 shillings. Printed shawls on muslin or fine wool could cost up to

£2 each. One advertisement in the Norwich Mercury for William Eastwood, linen draper and shawl manufacturer in 1825 reads as follows

'Elegant silk shawls, turnover, hand kerchiefs, shawl borders.
Scarf ends of every colour in shawls, every breadth in borders.'

Services advertising the refurbishment of shawls, offered

'Newly bordered, fringed and cleaned to look equal to new.'

Plain sections in shawls which showed signs of wear were replaced by a newly woven piece, or damaged sections could be cut out and the borders repositioned. Long shawls had end borders sewn onto adjacent sides to make them square. Ordinary washing was damaging to shawls and professional cleaners advertised their dry cleaning services.

Shawls were used to express sentiment, given at marriage as tokens of true love and on the birth of a child. In Scotland after a baby's birth, it became customary for a mother to wear a blue and cream woven shawl for the Churching ceremony. It also appears to have been a custom when a mother died, for her shawl to be cut in half for two of her female relatives. Family shawls were carefully stored to preserve them in special sandalwood, or cedar-wood boxes. Royal and high-born ladies made gifts of their shawls to ladies-in-waiting and younger friends or favoured servants.

The fashionable lady owned a selection of shawls from which to choose for special social occasions, changing seasons and for everyday wear. Varying qualities of warm and lightweight shawls were woven and hand-printed for winter and summer. Magazine engravings of scenes from the Great Exhibition in 1851 show public spectators in many of the galleries and nearly every lady wears a shawl. Fashion advised ladies to control their shawls by pinning their arms against their bosoms, which gave the contemporary desired effect of primness and respectability,

By the 1870s shawl-wearing was waning. Mass produced shawls from Paisley had flooded onto the market, making them cheaply available to the general public. With everybody owning them, the elite quickly rejected shawl-wearing as no longer fashionable. Also styles of dress were changing with huge skirts being replaced by the bustle. This hump-like construction at the back of the skirt was not as attractive for shawl display as the crinoline had been. But perhaps the real reason was that in the late 1870s, the fertile seeds of women's liberation were beginning to show in society; sport was being played (ladies in bustles were rushing around tennis courts), girls schools were founded and, despite warnings from the clergy that their ability to have children was being put at risk, girls were cycling. The former helpless dependent woman, was no longer an acceptable icon of feminine virtue and the wearing of a shawl was a restriction to these newly found freedoms.

The Norfolk Museums and Archaeology Service has a comprehensive collection of some of the finest of Norwich shawls made in the City, which can be viewed by appointment.

THE NORWICH SHAWL MANUFACTURER

For many hundreds of years the city of Norwich was renowned for its worsted cloth industry. As with all manufacturing trades it experienced times of great demand for its products and at others suffered from adverse influences on both its foreign and home markets. After a run of exceptional demand for 'Norwich stuffs' during the middle years of the 18th century, the closing decades saw a sharp decline due to loss of markets through wars, changes in fashion and other events beyond the control of the manufacturers. It was also a time when many significant inventions were radically changing the traditional ways of spinning and weaving by hand, resulting in fierce opposition from the workers for fear of losing their employment. Many of these new inventions required coal or fast flowing water to power them, both of which Norwich lacked.

It was the rising fashion for wearing shawls which partly came to the rescue. Quality shawls appealed to the fashionable world and the Norwich manufacturers, with their reputation for high quality products, were well placed to satisfy the demand. As demand increased many shawl makers with too little capital and experience jumped on the bandwagon, causing the inevitable fall in prices ending in some cases in bankruptcy. However, by the 1830s trade had recovered and it was during the next twenty years that some of the most individual and beautiful shawls were produced in Norwich.

There could be political handicaps too for the manufacturers; one threatened in 1807. Custom and Excise officers applied a new statute that a shawl of one yard square ceased to be a 'handkerchief' and became a 'garment', so was subject to more tax. The Norwich manufacturers complained and their case was taken up by the local Members of Parliament who were able to get the Board of Trade to rescind the statute. Interesting, as by this time, the fashionable shawl was indeed a garment!

Unfortunately hardly any records of the shawl-makers have survived, except where their names are listed in the business directories or in census returns. The most interesting references come from contemporary newspapers;

John Harvey 1755-1842
Mayor of Norwich 1792

Below Left:

Trade Tokens
Issued by John Harvey

A weaver at his loom.
Reverse: the Arms of the
City of Norwich.

Below right:
The Harvey Manufactory,
Colegate, Norwich.

reports in The Norwich Mercury and The Norfolk Chronicle, who catered for their readers' obvious interest in the achievements of the city's textile industry. In Norwich there was an elite of top families, who had been recognised for many decades as hands-on master craftsmen and who, at the end of the 18th century, were becoming known as manufacturers. In the 19th century, increasing wealth allowed some heads of businesses to live off private incomes, distance themselves from practising their crafts, and move into other professions, the law and notably banking. Manufacturers, also calling themselves shawl-makers, made it their business to know of trends in contemporary fashions through their London agents, and were well aware of the rising interest in Kashmiri shawls.

Alderman John Harvey, one of the most successful of these manufacturers was head of a long established firm of master-weavers; he had been commended in 1788 by the Society of Arts for weaving a yarn so fine that no other manufacturer would attempt it. In a letter to the Secretary of the Society, the Alderman refers to the yarn spun by a local spinner

> '....it equals in fineness of thread, the yarn of which Indian shawls are made,
> but it bears no comparison to its softness and silkiness.
> In the manufactory of shawls which I have invented, my constant endeavour
> has been to procure wool sufficiently soft.'

It is clear that he was aware of the demand for shawls and that the problem of matching the quality of the Indian shawls had to be overcome.

Alderman Harvey became associated with Philip J. Knights who appears to have been excellent at self-promotion from the many adverts and references by him in the Norwich Mercury. We do not know what their business relationship was, but both came to prominence in the Society of Arts for their work. Knights won a silver medal for producing counterpanes, and with John Harvey, gained the nation's notice in 1792, by presenting a Royal counterpane to King George III and Queen Charlotte. The counterpane measures 12ft. square, is woven in one piece without a seam and has a large embroidered centre with the Royal Arms and four deep borders of stylised flowers. (For details, see chapter on The Royal Counterpane)

In 1793 Philip Knights was appointed 'Shawlman to Her Majesty' and on the 12th December 1793 the Norwich Mercury records

> '....Queen Charlotte and the Princesses appeared in Shawl Dresses
> of Mr. Knight's manufacture.'

Knights had showrooms in London and in 1794 he mounted a very grand show called 'The Norwich Shawl Manufactory Exhibition at 136 Bond Street in honour of Her Majesty's birthday, and in the Strand at 'Knights Norwich Shawl manufactory', a display including

> '......in front of the house, were formed a pyramid of lamps;
> at the windows were seen little children embroidering shawls

Train up a Child in the way it should go

UNDER THE PATRONAGE

OF HER MAJESTY

And when old departs from it.

P. I. KNIGHT'S
Shawl Manufacturer
To her Majesty
No 2 Colgate Street S. Georges
NORWICH
349 Strand London

Shawls demd to look
Shawl Bed furniture
Dresses Scarfs Shawls & Fancy Waistcoats.
equal with New

under festoons of white and gold;
and in the centre was placed a beautiful model of a State bed.'

Knights also had a shop in fashionable Bath, where he showed;

'an Elegant Assortment of Ladies' Train Dresses,
Scarffs, Shawls, Sashes, Cravats and Gentlemen's Waistcoats.'

The square shawls, still hand embroidered, cost from 4 to 6 guineas'

Another partnership was formed in 1795 between Richard Bidwell and John Jarrold 'to make Shawls for the Shawl, Scarf and Waistcoat Shapes Trade.' Bidwell appears to have been the active partner and although a small firm, by the end of the century appear to be doing well, as he wrote to John Jarrold

'Our Shawl trade is wonderfully brisk.
Have now 18 looms at work and could employ three or four times as many.'

The partnership was dissolved in 1811.

In 1803 at Norwich Quarter Sessions, wages were fixed in favour of shawl weavers, as distinct from weavers of other fabrics.

In 1804 the Norwich Mercury states with pride

'Norwich manufactured shawls are in such high repute
that one manufacturer in the city has received an order for not less than
40,000.
Such an order must necessarily give employment to a great number of
men, women and children.'

After the difficult years of the 1820s there was a resurgence in the textile trade in the 1830s. Demand for fashionable shawls continued to grow and over the next twenty to thirty years the delightful colours and designs produced in Norwich confirm the taste and expertise of the shawl makers.

To market shawls, in addition to a local clientele, some manufacturers opened retail outlets in London and employed agents in the capital who advised them on fashion changes. Royal and aristocratic patronage was eagerly sought and the large drapery firm of Caley Bros., first noted in 1857 in London Street, Norwich, was appointed 'Shawlman to Her Majesty the Queen' in 1862. Changes in fashion was a constant hazard; a royal death was a significant event, meaning general mourning and the sudden halt to the wearing of colourful shawls. It could have an immediate and sometimes costly effect on orders in hand. To meet the Victorian cult of mourning, shawls in muted colours of black and lavender were popular.

At the beginning of the 19th century as the demand for shawls rose rapidly, an increasing number of small manufacturers had set up as shawl makers. Too much competition sent prices down and many were forced to close leaving only the well established firms. According to references in journals and newspapers, by 1851 and the year of the Great Exhibition, five Norwich manufacturers, in addition to making a variety of materials, were successful in selling shawls; Edward Blakely, Clabburn, Sons and Crisp, Grouts, E. & F. Hinde and Towler & Campin *(further details in appendix)*

By the 1870s fashions were changing and society's demand for shawls was declining sharply. After nearly one hundred years of successfully pleasing the *beau monde* with beautiful and desirable shawls, shawl making in the city was coming to an end.

Abel Towler 1842-1869 and his wife Elizabeth (late Campin)

This shawl is similar in design and colour to the shawl which was made by Towler, Rowling and Allen for the City of Norwich to present to Queen Victoria when she visited Norwich in 1869.

Shawls by Abel Towler, at various times in partnership with
Campin: Shickle: Matthews: Rowling: Allen.

Many of Towler's designs were registered with the Public Registration Office in the 1840s

Shawls by Clabburn Sons and Crisp 1851 to 1863 (overleaf)

The Clabburn shawls of the 1860s were woven on Jacquard looms.

They were made of silk, and on average measure 3.5m. by 1.5m.,

with designs of similar motifs

and are superbly woven.

Fashion was changing

and they are the final flowering of the

shawl-wearing fashion.

SHAWLS BY E. & F. HINDE

A Style of shawl called an ARAB in Norwich and a GLASGOW in Paisley was popular from the 1840s: printed on silk leno they were large and semi-circular at one end: E. & F. Hinde seem to have specialised in printing them as in their order book dated 1847/8 sales of 33 different types of ARAB shawls are listed - unknown styles now.

1870s

block printed detail on silk leno ARAB   1866

DESIGNING NORWICH SHAWLS

Quality shawls, with patterns of elegance and style were woven and printed for an elite clientele, confirming their wealth and status in society. Over the years of catering for an exclusive market, Norwich shawls developed a distinctive and attractive character, in their designs and colourings.

As the fashion for shawl wearing took hold, other weaving centres in Scotland and France were soon fiercely competing and manufacturers were freely copying traditional Indian designs for the rapidly expanding European market. Eastern designs were richly coloured, using stylised floral and plant forms, and particularly with a motif known as the *boteh* (Hindi for flower) which figured in nearly all the Indian designs. This motif, over the century changed its form and appeared in many variations, as designers made new interpretations of the classic shape by altering the proportions of the *boteh*, its decorative fillings and surrounding borders. These alterations in the patterned 'galleries' at the shawl ends, the side borders and ground details changed to suit the fashions of the day.

Today, we know the *boteh* as the *paisley* design. During the 19th century, fine quality shawls were produced in this Scottish town, but as Paisley's manufacturers increased their mass production of shawls, cheaper versions reached a wider class of society and quality was often sacrificed. Until around 1840, Edinburgh had been a significant weaving centre and from the end of the 18th century until production declined, had made high quality shawls. When large shawls came into fashion, especially Jacquard woven silks, several important centres in France excelled in producing magnificent shawls. Norwich made quality the priority in their shawl making, and continued to use the draw-loom to make fine cloth decorated with distinctive patterns and colours, at prices the wealthy were prepared to pay.

The origins of the *boteh* are uncertain; one theory is that it is the printed shape of the base of a clenched fist, another links it to the heart of the date palm. It would seem likely that the design came to India from Persia in the 16th century in the stylised form of a dianthus flower, with two small buds on either side and leaves, held in a little vase, or tied with a bow. This neat arrangement, with its leaves at the top turning to one side, was gradually stylised into the *boteh* motif. In Norwich the design was known as the *pine* and in France was called the *palme*. There are very few shawls which do not

VARIATIONS

IN

THE

DEVELOPMENT

OF

THE

BOTEH

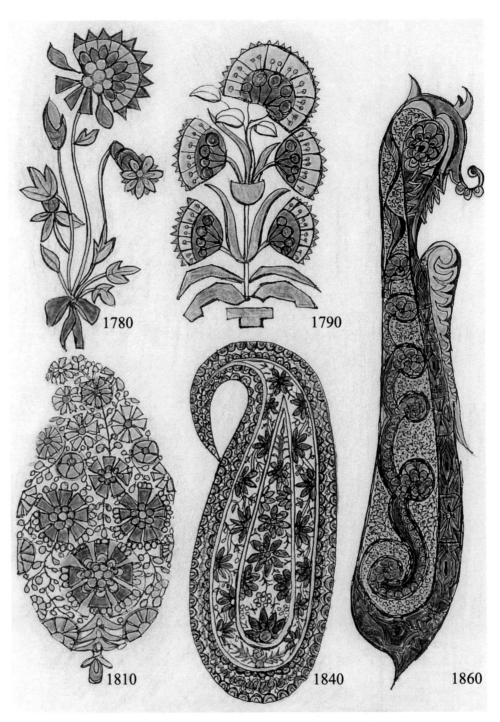

1780

1790

1810

1840

1860

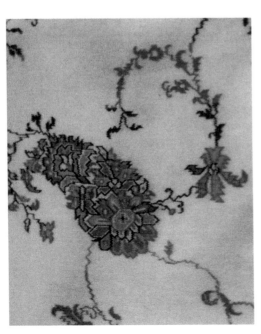

have variations of this distinctive motif. During the 19th century, the development of the *boteh* can be traced from rather plump motifs with simple floral fillings, to huge elongated complex vegetal, geometric and Gothic forms, which reflected the changing styles of the time. Other art forms of the 19th century, furnishings, ceramics, were decorated with similar stylised forms. For researchers, the shapes, sizes and fillings of the *boteh* design offer clues in dating shawls.

Little is known of the designers of the Norwich shawls. In census records and business directories a few pattern drawers are recorded, but it is uncertain if they were creative designers or just capable draughtsmen whose job was to prepare designs for the looms. At the end of the 18th century, it is likely that a manufacturer would have obtained an imported Indian shawl and given it to his in-house pattern drawer/draughtsmen to copy and work out the design for embroidery or the loom. Draughtsmen with talent and flair would have been encouraged to introduce their own ideas, but there is evidence that it was the manufacturers who, knowing what suited their market, kept a firm hand on the pattern making. Some free-lance designers, usually based in London, travelled with designs and called on manufacturers with their portfolios. Designers working in London often in studios, were more in touch with changes in fashions, especially those coming from France, which, as the century passed was the centre of fashion. Prominent Norwich manufacturers had London agents who advised them on the current styles demanded by the fashionable world.

Some contemporary pattern books have survived; in these, manufacturers kept their collection of paper designs and in some, a difference in the expertise of the hand of the pattern maker producing the designs is obvious. One such pattern book in use during the 1830s, contains a design collection of the Norwich shawl manufacturer Richard Shaw, has been acquired by the Norfolk Museums and Archaeology Service and the contents have been invaluable for identifying shawls woven by this maker. Designs in the Shaw collection, have confirmed the style of fashionable shawls of that period. Some of the papers have the names of the weavers who wove the shawls written in and a grid has been pencilled on certain paper patterns to show how the loom was to be set up.

In the 1840's there was national concern about the poor quality of commercial design and schools of design were established. Local manufacturers supported a scheme to set up a textile design department in the newly opened Norwich Technical School. However, there was universal disappointment when the schools insisted on students being trained to make drawings from antique sculpture but offered no understanding or training in the practical problems of designing for industry; unlike the French, who continued to train their designers specifically for the textile industry.

Another problem for the manufacturers was piracy of designs. In a report to A Commission to Report into the Conditions of Hand Loom Weavers in 1839, evidence was given by weavers that, because a shawl was a fashion

Obadiah Short 1803-1886
Designer and Painter

Designs attributed to Obadiah Short

garment, the designs had to be changed frequently, which was time consuming and expensive. A Mr. Etheridge said that:

'...he had brought out a shawl of a most beautiful pattern and it was taking well and yielding a good profit; but he had just received a letter from his London agent telling him that the pattern had been imitated by the Scotch and advising him to discontinue it immediately.'

he added;

'When the Scotch take up a pattern they inundate the market with such abundance that the article becomes quite common and ladies of property will not buy a shawl of which there are many imitations.'

After representations from the manufacturers, the Government set up the registration of designs at the Public Registration Office and a manufacturer could pay six pence or a shilling which protected a design for three or six months. Of all the manufacturers in Norwich between 1842 and 1875, only seven appear to have registered their designs. There are 315 designs in the Public Registration Office, both woven and printed. Copies of some registered designs by Norwich manufacturers have been obtained by the Norfolk Museums and Archaeology Service and are an invaluable source, against which shawls can be dated and linked to a manufacturer.

One designer was Obadiah Short who was born in Norwich in 1803. At an early age he was employed to fill bobbins for a weaver, he then trained to weave bombazine cloth and later, became recognised for his oil and water-colour paintings of local scenes. In the 1851 census he is listed as a 'designer' and is known to have worked for fifty years as a 'pattern drawer' for the shawl manufacturers Willett and Nephew. There is an example of an 1860 shawl design in the Norfolk Museums and Archaeology Service collection, by Obadiah Short, but unfortunately there is no record of the designs he made for Willett. He had a son, also named Obadiah, who is listed in the 1851 census as a 'designers assistant'.

Another named designer was John Funnell who seems to have worked as a free-lance. He designed the pattern for the superbly woven, silk jacquard shawl which Messrs. Clabburn, Son and Crisp entered for the Paris Exposition in 1862. It was awarded a gold medal, but due to internal dissention and protests from the competing French manufacturers, the gold was withdrawn and only a silver medal was awarded. This did not go down well in Norwich. The shawl, which is in the museum collection, is typical in size (three metres by one and a half) to suit the large skirts of the time. The designs at the two deep end borders are arranged in the so-called 'scissor' pattern, filled with scrolls and complex floral details. The style often appears at this time and would seem to anticipate the designs of the Art Nouveau movement of the 1890s.

These great shawls of the 1860's were influenced in pattern and colour by French designers. British manufacturers would visit studios to buy French

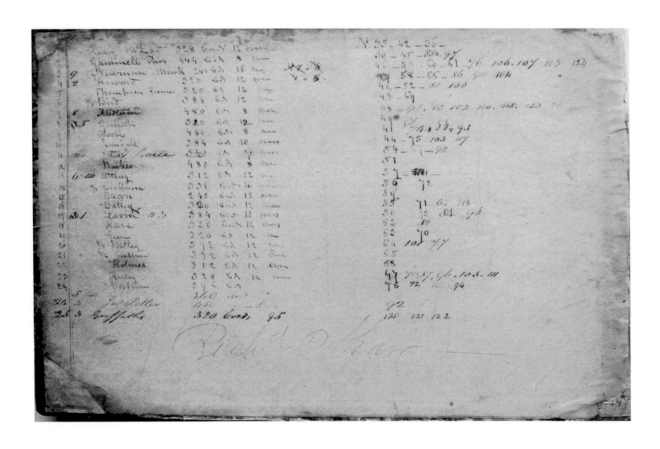

The Richard Shaw Norwich Shawl Pattern Book in the collection of
the Norfolk Museums and Archaeology Service at Carrow House, Norwich.

THE RICHARD SHAW PATTERN BOOK 1832

This gouach design,

overlaid

with a hand drawn grid,

was used to

set up the loom

for the weaving of

the shawl

depicted below.

Turnover shawl c 1832

made using the

'*Fillover*' technique

from

silk and wool

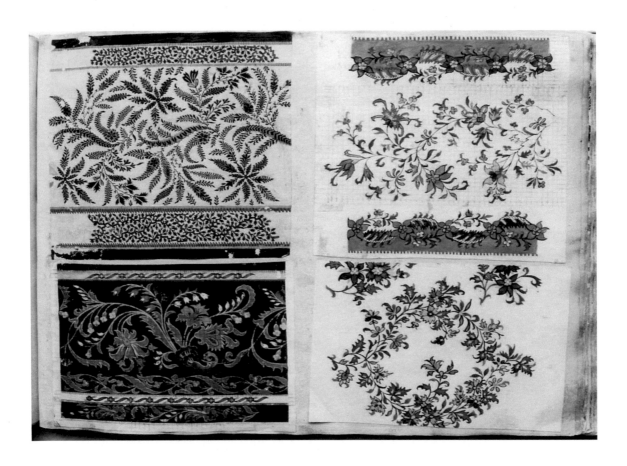

Richard Shaw's Pattern Book - designs for shawl borders, some on point paper

designs and, such is the similarity in style, that at this period it becomes difficult to be certain which centre had manufactured the shawl, unless the design has been registered. Unlike in Britain, the work of French designers was preserved and it is possible to see in the Musée National des Techniques in Paris, the signed pencil and gouach designs on paper which were made for a section of a shawl (repeated in four quarters on the loom) by prominent designers such as Amédée Couder and Antony Berrus.

By the end of the 1860s mass produced shawls, which were often coarse, heavy and 'muddy' in colour, had robbed shawl-wearing of its prestige. The designs of *boteh*, *pines* and *palmes*, with arabesques of swirling, inter-twining stylised floral-filled patterns, had become clichés and shawls were going out of favour.

The motif however, has never been forgotten and reappears from time to time in textile design. Dressing gowns, dress materials, ties etc. use it and it is universally called the *paisley*. Perhaps, if Norwich had been as good at promoting shawls, as it was at making them, the motif might now be known as the *norwich!*

Shawls with links to known Designers

John Funnell 'scissor' design, popular in 1862

William Morrison 1848

George Vincent (possibly) 1860

Variations of the BOTEH motif from floral to geometric.

1815

1820

1860

Early Embroidered Shawls

The Little Shawl Worker
by Joseph Clover 1815
Engraved by Thomas Overton 1825

Patterns on early shawls
were darned into the fabric

NORWICH SHAWL WEAVERS

By the end of the 18th century, the city's old weaving practices had changed very little. In crowded conditions, weavers were home-workers in parishes around Magdalen Street across to Pottergate and over the river Wensum. There was a strong community life; the Norwich weaver was known for his independence of mind and had a fine reputation for taking pride in his craftsmanship. When trade was good, pay compared well with workers on the land, and rates for shawl weaving were better than for plain cloth weavers.

Cloth-making in the North of England was being rapidly mechanised and factory working there was soon to become the norm. Despite increasing competition, Norwich weavers saw the new practices as a threat to their working and community life and were resistant to change. In the late 18th and early 19th century, society's demand for beautiful and individual shawls was being met by the Norwich masters and shawl weavers, who continued to use their traditional practices. Some manufacturers who tried to change from drawloom to Jacquard weaving in the 1830s, met opposition from the weavers and Jacquard looms were not used to make shawls until the 1850s.

A boy started a seven year weaving apprenticeship with a master at fourteen years of age. After qualifying as a journeyman he could work for other masters. Ambitious men with capital set up as master weavers and employed out-reach workers. During the industry's golden years in the 18th century, master weavers had built large residences in the city from which they conducted their business. Here, work was given out and on its return the worker was paid; shawls were then finished and marketing was arranged.

Weavers worked in their homes at drawlooms (often hired); conditions were cramped, but as long as shawls were delivered promptly they could work in their own time. After the warp of the loom had been prepared, weaving began, with a drawboy in charge of a system of cords attached to the loom. The weaver sent shuttles filled with coloured yarn across the warp, while calling out instructions to the boy to pull the numbered cords, so creating the patterned cloth. When work was complete and the shawl had been cut from the loom, surplus yarns on the back were clipped off by hand, later this task was done by machine.

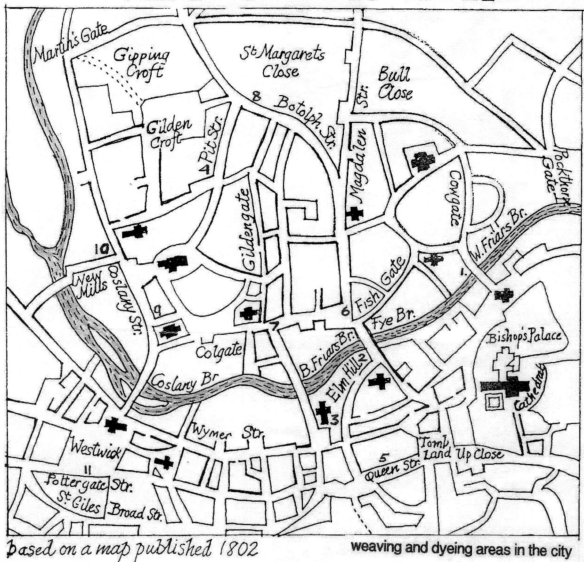

CITY of NORWICH

based on a map published 1802

weaving and dyeing areas in the city

Manufacturers

1. Yarn Factory, St. James
2. Towler & Campin
3. J.H. Allen
4. Clabburn Sons & Crisp
5. Edward Blakely
6. C.F. Bolingbroke
7. Richard Shaw
8. Geary & Sultzer
9. Grout & Co.
10. E. & F. Hinde
11. Willett & Nephew

Street scene near the church of St. Lawrence
by Henry Ninham

A weaver was paid according to the number of skeins of weft yarn used. Annually, Justices of the Peace reviewed the rates paid and any adjustments if considered necessary were then made. Some manufacturers defied the Justices' rulings: in 1809 the Norwich Mercury reported that a journeyman Thomas Harmer, complained that a master, John Thompson should have paid him £6. 3. 4 for weaving a shawl, but had only given him 4 guineas. At the Michaelmas Quarter Sessions Thompson was fined ten shillings, but the Court held that they were not allowed by law to insist that Harmer was paid the arrears. John Thompson argued that he could not afford to pay the wages agreed by the Justices. The Attorney General was consulted for his advice and commented, apparently on the side of the weaver; 'As the evil is increasing and is a very serious one for the journeyman, the Magistrates are desirous of supporting them all they can, particularly as their conduct has been remarkably temperate and proper'. Sadly it seems that Thomas Harmer was the loser; he had to take time off for the hearing, as did his two witnesses who had vouched for Thompson's refusal to pay, but there was no compensation for lost time. The Attorney General advised that Harmer could apply to the Court of Common Law for retribution; this would incur further expense and loss of time. It meant that without financial backing workers were unable to fight for their rights.

Conditions deteriorated; angry crowds gathered, violence broke out, manufacturers and their premises were attacked. Those masters who had sent yardage weaving out to the surrounding villages where cheaper rates were paid, were particular targets of the weavers' wrath. The workers searched wagons coming into the city and in one instance unbridled the horse and set fire to the cloth and cart.

In 1822 the Norwich Mercury stated that Yorkshire goods were cheaper and that unless weavers' wages were lowered manufacturers would not be able to compete. The Committee of Journeymen Weavers issued a statement that it would be impossible for families to survive. They went on to state the needs of a hypothetical family of a bombazine weaver (the rates for weaving bombazine were lower than those for shawl weaving) which gives an indication of how families spent their income.

Working twelve hours a day in three weeks he can weave two pieces for £2. 5. 0. which is fifteen shillings per week.

His wife filled his quills so there is no charge for this, but his outgoings for a week for six people will be as follows:

Winding on, twistering on, shuttle, pickers and cord		6d.
Rent	2s.	6d.
Firing the year round	1s.	6d.
Meat, three quarters of a pound a day	2s.	2d.
Bread	4s.	0d.
Flour, half a stone	1s.	2d.
Beer, one pint a day	1s.	6d.
Butter, half a pint		8d.
Cheese, half a pound		4d.
Milk, one pint		9d.

James Churchyard b. c1833 d. 1913: worked all his life as a weaver

Woven in 1860 when James was employed by Clabburn Sons and Crisp .

Tea, one ounce		*5d.*
Sugar, half a pound		*4d.*
Sauce	*1s.*	*0d.*
Soap, candles and oil, year round	*1s.*	*0d.*
Salt, pepper, vinegar and sundries		*4d.*
For bedding, clothing, etc.	*1s.*	*0d.*

. Total   18s. 11d   Income 15s.

There is 3/11d. going out more than coming in – let anyone judge

Some weavers had small gardens and later the council offered allotments to help 'feed poor families'. Living in crowded conditions health was poor, often from drinking contaminated water, infant mortality was high and some families were wretchedly housed. In 1845, 2,500 persons are recorded on 'out-relief' in the city and three quarters of them were weavers. There was a meagre poor law and finally the workhouse.

In 1849 a press reporter visited the homes of some of the cloth workers to find out exactly what their lives were like. One of the best weavers had been commissioned to make a shawl for the famous singer Jenny Lind, known as the 'Swedish Nightingale', who often sang in Norwich. The weaver told the reporter that it took him five weeks to prepare the loom for the shawl and he was employed for three-quarters of the year making other shawls of the same pattern. On the same warp he could make one shawl per week for which he was paid 24s. 10d. Out of that he had to pay the winder 2s. 6d., his drawboy 7s., for picking 6d., the hire of the loom 2s. 6d., and the cost of three candles at 4d. each. These items added up to 13s. 6d. leaving 11s. 4d. for his week's work. He told the reporter Miss Lind had been very kind and had sent round to ask if there was anything he needed. He said he wanted nothing as he thought it would be imposing on her, but as she insisted he must have something, his daughter suggested he needed a greatcoat. Miss Lind agreed and sent a tailor to measure him and subsequently provided the weaver with a coat, the like of which he had not had for many years.

As fashionable shawls increased in size and designs became more complex and detailed, they were more suited to be made on a loom equipped with a Jacquard shedding mechanism, requiring only one person to operate it. Cards punched with a series of holes, according to which warp threads required lifting to form the shed for the detailed stylised flowers and vegetal forms, replaced the services of the drawboy and greatly speeded up production. Some of the very fine yarns used for warps needed the application of a dressing, usually made from starch, to help resist friction in the loom. Colouring selective areas of a warp was sometimes used to enhance designs, requiring a very skilful weaver able to precisely control his rhythm and beat.

Adoption of the use of Jacquard mechanisms on top of the four poster looms meant, because of the increase in height, looms could no longer be accommodated in weavers houses and had to be housed in workshops and purpose built factories.

As fashion changed the demand for shawls fell, some manufacturers invested in new enterprises such as boot and shoe making and many former textile workers found employment in this new fast growing industry.

However, some weavers continued to work independently. William Arms worked in Barrack Street and was known as a competent shawl weaver. His niece remembered watching him carrying his beam with his finished work on his shoulder to his masters in St. Clement's Alley (C. & F. Bolingbroke & Jones).

James Churchyard worked as a weaver all his life; he died in 1913 aged 82 having worked for several masters. He started weaving shawls using a drawloom, but later used looms fitted with Jacquard mechanisms. His great niece donated four of his shawls to the Norfolk Museums and Archaeology Service. They are very varied, each reflecting the style of the time and the firm he worked for. One is clearly a Clabburn, Sons & Crisp design, but with a different colouring to a shawl in the museum's collection. James Churchyard was also well known for making 'wrappers'; these were 90cm patterned silk squares for gentlemen's neck wear on the hunting field. It was said that James was a crusty character who would only work for the firms he approved of!

Pamela Clabburn wrote:

'The Norwich weaver was nothing if not accomplished.
He might be and often was, obstinate and averse to change,
but he was a competent and often brilliant weaver who loved his home,
his tiny garden and his Norwich canary, and produced some wonderful
shawls.'

Jacquard woven shawls of the late 1860s.

 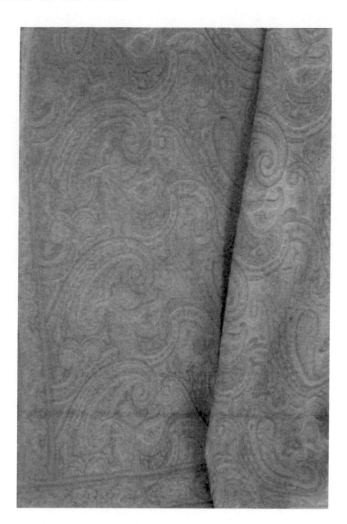

Two shawls woven by William Arms

Printed Shawls

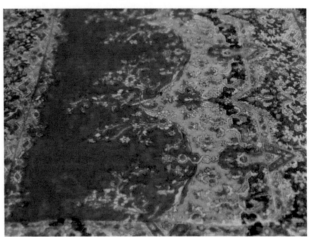

Harriet Ann Dickenson c1857

1840s to 1860s

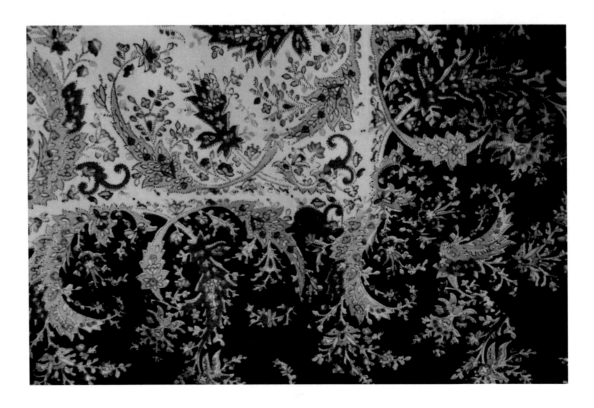

DYEING AND PRINTING

Nineteenth century Norwich dyers gained a good reputation for the quality of dyes used in weaving and printing shawls. The bright colours they produced could be depended upon not to fade in light or during cleaning and for this reason much cloth and yarn from other textile areas was sent to the city to be dyed. Red dyes were highly prized, particularly one which came to be known as 'Norwich Red'.

Archaeological excavations (*East Anglian Archaeology Report No. 17 1983*) uncovered evidence of ancient dyeing along the river Wensum. Quantities of seeds from the tenth century *reseda lueola*, commonly called dyers rocket which gives a bright fast yellow have been found. In the 13th and 14th centuries fine red worsted cloth was in great demand; red was a status colour and specialist red-dyer's skills could produce a brilliant unadulterated dye. Red dye was obtained from the root of the madder plant *rubria tinctoria*, which was grown locally and is recalled today in Norwich in a church and street called St. John Maddermarket where the dye was once sold. Later, stronger madder was imported from the continent, then from Turkey. The ancient British woad *isatis tinctoria* grown locally, gave a blue dye, later replaced by imported indigo. Many other plants, lichens, berries, insects, molluscs, woods and metals were worked to make dyes which gave the dyer a broad palette of colours, some being faster to light and washing than others.

From the 1850s onwards, many of these naturally sourced dyes were overtaken and discarded when synthetic dyes were discovered. Until then, the craft of dyeing was considered an Art whose success depended on the experience, knowledge and skill of the master dyer, but with the change to synthetic dyes, accurate formulae defining the composition of the dyes and dyeing were controlled by the chemist. Not only was the dyeing of textiles changed by synthetically made colour, but artists working in oils and water colours had new and exciting ranges of colours available for their palettes.

As they had done since medieval times, Norwich 19th century dyers worked in dye houses situated in little lanes running down to and along the river Wensum, giving access to the vast quantities of water required for the various dyeing processes. Conditions in the dye-houses made the job hard for labourers and it was well known that few lived to an old age. Subjected to constant steamy wet conditions, they lifted heavy lengths of cloth or poles

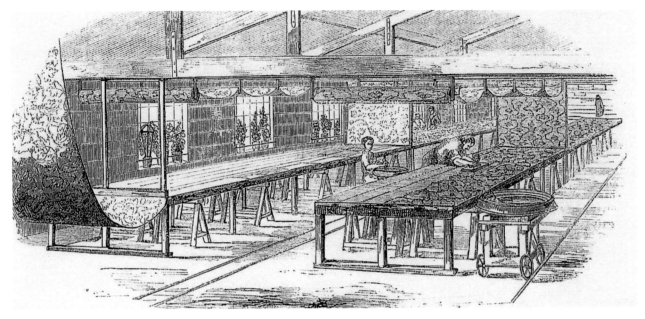

Printing yardage (note 'tear' or tierboy' on left): from
The Illustrator, Exhibitor and Magazine of Art

Below:

Later development of hand blocks

Brass and copper pins and wire were
hammered into the wood to make the
detailed printing surfaces required
for the 1830s designs.

A separate block was required for each colour
in the design: wooden blocks were made of
three layers of wood which were fixed together
to withstand repeated use, the design was
carved on the top layer: blocks were struck
with a heavy 'maul' or printer's mallet, which
transferred the dye to the fabric.

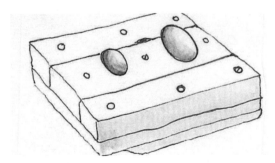

The underside of the wooden block showing
thumb and finger holes for the printer to grip.
Blocks were limited to 10lbs. weight.

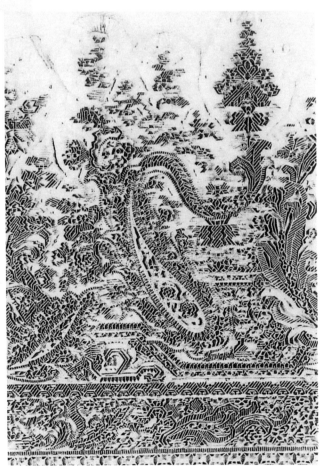

laden with yarn from vats of boiling dyes, transferring them to large tubs or becks, some 6½ ft. deep, with constant changes of cold water for the frequent rinses that silks and woollens required. Mordants were needed to fix dyes and many were dangerous to lungs and skin, but there was little or no protection for the worker against the toxic materials needed in the dyeing processes. Acids, such as sulphuric; minerals, chrome, lead, nitrate, copper and salts, sodium chloride, caustic soda and ammonia with many other hazardous materials were required to make dyes that were brilliant, fast to light and washing. One example of the dangers of these dyes comes in a report about 19th century dyers' conditions; it had been observed that their mouths, noses and hands had been eaten away by the action of chrome on their skin. The preparation of these substances and the processes carried out, would be inconceivable in our modern world.

Over the years, newspapers and journals offer glimpses of the dyers' achievements. The Norwich Mercury reported

'By the middle of the 18th century the dyers of Norwich had become pre-eminently known for the beauty of their dyeing so that worsted textures were forwarded from all parts of England to be dyed'.

From 1783 the number of dyers listed in the Norwich Trade Directories fluctuates. 'Scarlet Dyers' are recognised as being a separate branch; some dyers like J. Hannet offered cleaning services in 1815, that his establishment

'...cleans and dyes...fillover shawls, painted ditto and lace veils cleaned and dressed like new...'

The reference to 'painted' was a practice by printers in the early century, who employed women with paint brushes to follow the printer and pencil in small coloured areas of the design on the fabric while it was being printed on the table.

A Norwich dyer who was famous in his time was Michael Stark, the father of James, a well known member of the Norwich School of Painters. Michael was born in 1748 and came to Norwich from Scotland to join a firm of scarlet dyers, taking over the business in 1811. Aware of the action of chemical elements, among his many achievements was the introduction of chlorine gas to bleach cloth in controlled conditions. In association with Messrs. Sims and Pitchford, Michael Stark perfected the dyeing processes for making an excellent black and a very fine scarlet. The latter was an important development in red-dyeing, whereby both the silk and woollen yarns in woven cloth would dye exactly to the same shade of colour. Getting the same intensity of colour for mixed fibres had always been a problem for dyers and this was a break through. The dye came to be known as 'Norwich Red', its fame spread and for a long time, Norwich was the main supplier of dyed yarn used to make tartan cloth for the Scottish regiments.

When Michael Stark died on the 23rd February 1831 the obituary in the Mercury paid tribute to the contribution he had made to the wealth of the city

'Died this day at his house in Thorpe, Mr. Michael Stark aged 83. To Mr. Stark, Norwich was indebted for the introduction of many valuable discoveries and improvements which tended considerably to the success of its manufacturers.'

His eldest son William took over as head of the business and was active politically when the textile industry experienced hard times. With the great advances that the invention of synthetic colours brought, he was closely involved with the changes they brought to the traditional practices of dyeing. At his death in 1863, he was described in his obituary as

'one of the most eminent chemists of his day and particularly distinguished as one of the foremost dyers of fabrics in Norwich manufacture'.

In *'A Companion to the Norwich Polytechnic Exhibition'* in 1840, where most of the foremost manufacturers had exhibited their finest shawls, a Mrs. Barwell wrote

'Another source of prosperity for Norwich was the excellence of its dyeing. Mr. Michael Stark devoted his life to improvements in the dyeing business; and the reputation of Norwich for excellent colours is mainly due to him and his sons. His eminence in the dyeing and dressing of bombazines brought nearly every piece in Kidderminster and Yorkshire to Norwich to be dyed.'

Mrs. Bardwell then testifies to the fact that recipes for dyeing, in company with paper designs, were subject to industrial espionage.

'To the disgrace of human nature, bribery and treachery were on foot to obtain secrets of the dyes and the villainy of a confidential servant deprived Messrs. Stark of the advantages they must have enjoyed.'

A dyer's recipe book was a cherished possession and he guarded his recipes from competitors. Notebooks recorded the quantities and mixtures of dyestuffs, mordents used, the number of times yarns were immersed and observations of practices which had resulted in a successful dye. K.G. Ponting in his Dictionary of Dyes and Dyeing (1961 p.58) recalls having heard it said that

'.....a dead cat was thrown into the dye-bath, whereupon things improved.'

Few recipe books have survived, as it seems to have been customary for a notebook to be destroyed on the death of a dyer. An interesting notebook dated 1862 is kept at the Bridewell Museum, Norwich. It belonged to an unknown dyer who worked for Messrs. E. and F. Hinde and contains his recipes for dye-baths, with his introduction of new synthetic dyestuffs which he combines with traditional natural stuffs. He records times for boiling and washing and in one recipe advises that

'...during the working time, add one glass of vitriol – the acid taste should always prevail.'

An indication that not only did the dyer use his eyes, but tasting too was needed when overseeing a dye-bath!

Little is known about the Norwich printers and the practices they used to print lightweight mixed yarns and silk leno shawls, often from designs that had been used to make woven shawls. Skill was required to fit wooden and metal blocks accurately onto the stretched cloth and build up patterns which made the overall complex designs of the large shawls that were fashionable in the 1860s. Cutting and making blocks was a trade in itself and few examples have survived; two in the Bridewell Museum show the change from the simple early wooden carvings of the early century, to the large intricate designs, made with the insertion of metal strips and dots into the blocks surface. Most shawl designs had six colours; a separate block was required for each and as the print images increased in size, the limit in weight for each block was fixed at ten pounds.

Printers worked with a tier-boy whose job was to cover the print side of the block with dye by pressing its surface to a dye impregnated blanket stretched over a drum of dye. Guided by registration marks made from outstanding pins on each block, the printer placed a block, starting with the lightest colour onto the fabric and struck it with his mallet. Looking at the back of a printed shawl, it is possible to judge the skill of a printer by the evenness of each block's printed image. Having blocks made for shawl-printing involved a heavy investment for the manufacturer, especially if design or colour fashion suddenly changed. Often shawls were printed by using design-borders in conjunction with centre motifs from earlier designs.

The 19th century dyers were skilful, knowledgeable and dedicated to their craft. Tribute must be paid to the quality of their work which today shows little change in the brilliance and permanence of the dyes they used to colour the old shawls.

NORWICH RED

Michael Stark's red dye was famous in
the 19th century.

Right: Madder plant, the root contains the dye.

Below: Lithograph by James Stark of his
father's dye works, situated at
Duke's Palace Bridge, Norwich, 1887.

Dye Works
Duke's Palace Bridge

Interior of Grout and Co. Dyehouse c1910-14

The working conditions of these men had little changed since the middle of the 19th century.

Bert Nichols, on the far right, was Assistant Manager: he died of tuberculosis in 1930.

The Great Exhibition

Crystal Palace

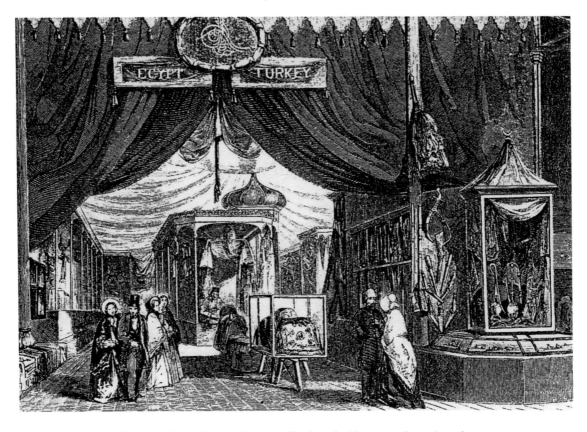

Engraving of one of the galleries: ladies wearing shawls

THE
GREAT
EXHIBITION

A unique opportunity was created in 1851 for manufacturers to show their work to the rest of the world. Initiated by Queen Victoria's husband, Prince Albert proposed inviting makers from all over Britain, the Colonies and the rest of the world to exhibit their work in London. The exhibition would show that by uniting art and industry the Industrial Revolution had brought success and benefit to the world. Hostility towards the proposal was met from many prominent people who argued that British manufacturing would be undermined by foreign competitors stealing their secrets. Despite the opposition and a lack of co-operation, the Prince's party persevered and money was raised. A building constructed of iron and glass designed by Joseph Paxton was erected in Hyde Park and became known as the Crystal Palace. When the exhibition opened in May, crowds flocked to see the large galleries filled with displays from all over the world. There was public wonder at the strangeness of many of the exhibits and some astonishment at the glimpses offered into unknown foreign cultures.

Amongst the myriad of exhibits from every craft and industry, textiles featured prominently. Foremost Norwich manufacturers Messrs. Towler and Campin, Clabburn Son & Crisp and Edward Blakely put the finest examples of their shawls and fabrics on display, receiving very favourable notices for the high quality of their work from contemporary critics.

Two publications accompanied the exhibition, *'An Illustrated Cyclopaedia of the Great Exhibition'* and the *'Art Journal Illustrated Catalogue'* . Among the many learned articles were *'The Harmony of Colour'* and *'A Lesson in Taste'*. Both publications give some fascinating opinions on the manufacturers and their shawls. For instance in an introduction to textiles *'The Art Journal'* comments

'The valuable and interesting display of British shawls was most judiciously arranged in the gallery of the south-western side of the transept, the London and Norwich contributions being placed in a series of elegantly designed glass cases'.

Engravings of the interior of the Crystal Palace depict the lofty galleries, with gentlemen in stovepipe hats and many ladies wearing large shawls over fashionable crinoline dresses.

By 1851 shawl wearing was at the height of its popularity, endorsed by the Queen who was known to be especially interested in acquiring the finest examples to wear. After the formal opening the Queen revisited the Exhibition and in her diary entry of 14th June she wrote

'Went first through one or two French courts and then upstairs to examine in detail the Norwich shawls of the lightest Cashmir material, also of silk with beautiful designs.'

'The Cyclopaedia' described many of the shawl exhibits, often critically, complaining that some makers had used harsh, crude colours, had not used complementary colours, or had overused the Pine motif. One shawl maker was reprimanded for not complying with contemporary taste by disregarding

'.....that most essential 'effect' of a shawl, to bring comfort and repose which has been disregarded. The blending of pattern and colours should be the prime consideration and the less out-of-the-wayism the better.'

Only a successful manufacturer could afford to set aside a working loom, weaver and the time required to make an exhibition shawl. The dressing of a draw or Jacquard loom to make a shawl of four yards in length and two yards in width could take several weeks to complete and it is likely that on the same warp six or seven shawls were made, with further weeks required to weave them. By altering the order of the weft colours on the same warp, each shawl would have had a different appearance and the manufacturer could then chose the most successful colour-way.

One such shawl received special notice in *'The Art Journal'* which published an engraved impression of part of the design.

'Messrs. Towler and Campin of Norwich exhibit some of the exquisite textile fabrics which have given character and reputation to this ancient city. A magnificent filover scarf (sic) is one of the contributions. It measures four yards in length and two in width. The sobriety in colour which prevails in these elaborate productions is a proof of the good taste of the manufacturer'.

Recently the Norfolk Museums and Archaeology Service has acquired one of these shawls; it is in perfect condition, beautifully woven with yarns which have lost none of their brilliance.

Edward Blakely's shawls were also favourably commented on. He had drawn attention to his work by displaying a Gold Shawl. On a black square of silk and worsted are deep patterned borders made of a bold design in strong colours. Notable was the gold-coated yarn (now rather faded) liberally woven into the background and design motifs. When on display the shawl must have glittered spectacularly. This shawl shows the strong influence of the famous

Towler & Campin at The Great Exhibition

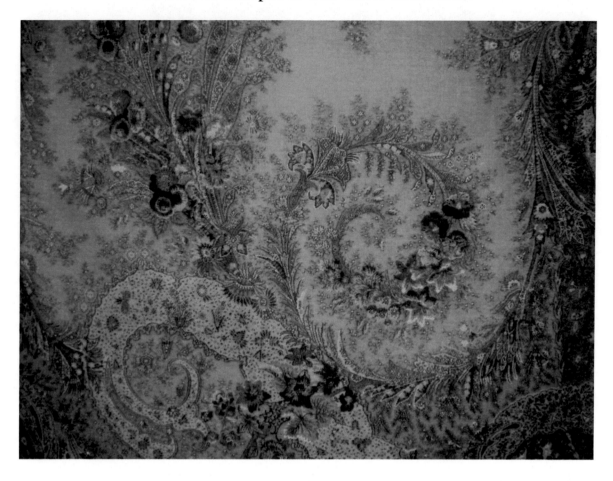

Towler & Campin displayed a shawl at The Great Exhibition: Norfolk Museums and Archaeology Service owns the above shawl which is believed to be the exhibited shawl.

An artist's engraved impression of part of the design which was published in The Art Journal and accompanied their appreciation and praise for Towler & Campin's entry in the Exhibition

Edward Blakely at The Great Exhibition

Edward Blakely entered a 'gold shawl' to draw attention to his stand at the Exhibition: the motifs were woven with gold covered yarn.

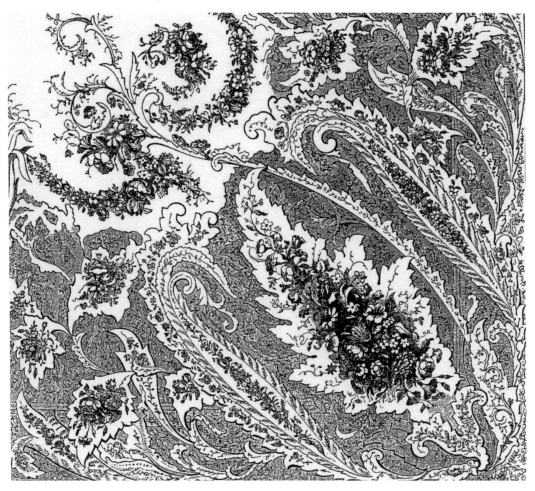

The Art Journal engraving of one of Blakely's shawls in the exhibition '...a tasteful arrangement, it is everything to be desired'.

designer Owen Jones whose similar designs appear in his *'Encyclopaedia of Design'* and it is possible that John Funnell who worked freelance for Mr. Blakely designed the shawl. Another of Mr. Blakely's shawls is featured in *'The Art Journal'* and includes an engraving of one corner of the shawl with the comment

'Mr. Blakely of Norwich contributes some splendid shawls woven expressly for the Exhibition. Space does not permit to enlarge on the beauty and merits it must be suffice to say they are the very best order of design, material and work.'

Messrs. Clabburn, Son and Crisp shawls were well represented by an engraving from 'The Cyclopaedia' with the comment

'....from a rich cashmere shawl manufactured by this firm in Norwich which we understand was purchased by the Queen. It is the first attempt in Norwich at shawl weaving on a Jacquard loom. For fineness of texture, variety and beauty of colours and elegance of pattern it cannot be surpassed.'

This is an interesting reference as it would seem that Messrs. Clabburn, Son and Crisp at that time were the only manufacturers in the city who were using Jacquard looms. To have a shawl purchased by the Queen was a considerable honour for the firm. They also entered poplins, brocades and hunting wrappers.

The Great Exhibition remained open from May to October, drawing over six million visitors to the Crystal Palace.

1820s possibly made by Willett & Nephew

1850 manufacturer John Sultzer

Detail of motif in shawl woven by James Churchyard

In 2009 an event was staged at Country & Eastern, Norwich
where privately owned Norwich Shawls were displayed on models.

Model wearing silk shawl c1825

1840s

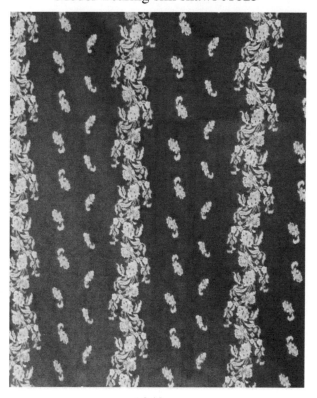

1840s

1858 turnover showing new synthetic red dye

1850s long shawl (3.5m. x 1.5m) in two colours to suit changeable wear

Model wearing c1862 large shawl displayed over fashionable crinoline.

1850　　　　　　　　　　　　　　　　　　　1870

Clabburn Sons & Crisp shawl woven in the Danish royal colours: a gift of a similar shawl
was presented to Princess Alexandra by the City of Norwich on her marriage to
Edward Prince of Wales in 1863.

The Royal Counterpane 1792

Right:
Embroidered
Centre of the
Royal Coat of
Arms

Below:
One of four
embroidered
borders with the
Royal Cypher
in the centre

THE ROYAL SHAWL COUNTERPANE

This remarkable textile apparently came into the Norwich Museum when it was founded, over a hundred years ago. The fabric had remained undisturbed and was stored in a very large box. Nothing was known of its origins. When Pamela Clabburn, then Curator of Strangers' Hall Museum, was clearing a storeroom, she saw – all covered in dirt, spiders' webs and dead flies –a large lump of fabric stuffed into a box. Curious to know what it was and to set about the cleaning, she undid the folds and spread them out. To her astonishment, the overall size stretched to twelve square feet; it was a seamless piece of cloth and in the centre was a large Royal coat of Arms. Pamela realised that the fabric was made of a silk warp with a wool weft, the whole piece surrounded by a silk fringe. In each corner were four shields with the Arms of England, Scotland, Ireland and France, all within a deep border of stylised roses, thistles, shamrocks and Garter Stars. These motifs were not woven into the fabric, but were embroidered in darning stitch. With mounting excitement Pamela recognised, in each corner of the border, the cipher of George III.

This was indeed an important textile with Royal connections and after much patient research into the eighteenth century records and particularly the Norwich Mercury and Norfolk Chronicle, Pamela discovered that in 1792 such a counterpane had been presented by the prominent Norwich manufacturer Philip John Knights, to King George III and Queen Charlotte for the Royal bed.

The condition of the counterpane was poor, not only was it ingrained with dirt but it was badly torn in places. Fund raising was organised and eventually the counterpane was sent to the conservation studio at Blickling. The fabric was professionally cleaned, repaired and stitched with vertical grid lines and nets to strengthen it. The counterpane is now stored with the rest of the costume and textile collection, at Carrow House.

There were no records accompanying the textile and it has been suggested that it might have been the prototype which allowed the manufacturer to be confident in the quality of his presentation. It could equally be the original counterpane which has, inexplicably, returned to Norwich. Perhaps its attribution will never be known, but as it seems to be the only one of its kind, the counterpane is a unique and valuable textile – especially for Norwich.

1830s
known as 'Chinese Architecture' Design

1860s

1840s

1850s

MODERN TIMES

THE STYLE AND SPLENDOUR EXHIBITION

Moving forward to 1995 when the Norfolk Museums and Archaeology Service staged a large exhibition of Norwich shawls at the Castle Museum.

Over one hundred examples of shawls made by Norwich manufacturers were displayed, accompanied by comprehensive accounts of working practices in the weaving, dyeing and printing industries. Vivienne Westwood, the well-known fashion designer, opened the exhibition; she spoke of her interest in past designers' work and the value of museum collections of designs by previous generations to provide inspiration for modern artists.

Many visitors came to the exhibition; some expressed their surprise that such magnificent textiles had actually been made in Norwich! It stimulated research and prompted families to find out more about older members who had worked in the industry.

One very elderly lady was able to describe her working day as a weaver before world war one; she was trained to weave puggarees (strips of material which were tied round pith helmets for wear in the tropics). Made of gauze she recalled each had a shawl pattern on the ends. When engaged to train as a weaver at age thirteen, she was taken on because her hands were dry and free of perspiration.

An elderly Norwich man whose grandparents had been employed in the textile industry examined the display on dyeing and the storyboards on Norwich Red carefully, before remarking

'I remember Mother saying the river always runs red in Norwich'.

Listening to visitors' observations it became clear that the practices of the old textile industry were beyond the experience and memory of all but a few of the very old.

The exhibition revived public interest and Norwich-made shawls began to be appreciated again. Since then, further research has brought new information about the manufacturers, and has stimulated interest in collecting Norwich shawls.

As sport and greater mobility

became popular

shawl-wearing

quickly declined.

POSTSCRIPT

It is remarkable that the fashion for wearing shawls lasted for nearly a century. From their first introduction as exotic accessories, worn with the daring dresses fashionable at the end of the 18th century, to the 1830s when shawls began to endow the wearers with the gentility that society aspired to. Wearing a shawl could give an air of angelic femininity to a lady and this was to last for sometime.

Early Victorian woman was prized for her self-effacing gentleness. An 1840s lady, tightly corseted, closely bonneted, arrayed in many petticoats (until the crinoline brought some relief) and cocooned in a shawl, was somewhat restricted in her movements and most appeared content that this was so. By the late 1860s the pace of change in society's modes and manners quickened and was reflected in contemporary fashions. The shape of skirts altered and no longer was it advantageous for retailers at the top end of the market to prominently display the exclusive, iconic shawls of the earlier years of the decade. Fashionable dress was flattening at the front of the skirt and a large 'hump', the bustle, appeared at the rear. This could often be displayed quite seductively and a constraining shawl arranged over a bustle, was much less attractive.

Styles of dress continued to define a woman's class and wealth, but as ready-to-wear clothes became increasingly available in the last quarter of the century, the boundaries of class were shifting. Mass production made it possible for the less affluent to own shawls and cheap patterned ones could be bought for weddings, christenings and special occasions. Owning a shawl now gave its wearer a sense of working-class pride.

By the end of the 19th century expensive shawls, previously highly regarded, were, by some families, carefully stored as valued family heirlooms. Many others were used as bedspreads, table covers, throws and curtains. Sadly some show damage from water stains or nail holes. Pamela Clabburn was somewhat annoyed to find a valuable silk and worsted shawl lining a dog's basket! More creatively, silk and worsted shawls were cleverly made into dresses, jackets, dressing gowns and housecoats.

Occasionally, high quality Norwich shawls come onto the market and can make a good sale price if the manufacturer is known and the shawl is in good condition. Their beautiful patterns and designs, and the technical excellence in weaving and dyeing, make them valuable works of art.

Strangely, the old shawls still seem to carry an aura of status about them.

Many family shawls
were stored, others were
made into garments
or used as
curtains,
table and bed
coverings.

20th century jackets made from 19th century shawls

Right: Housecoat made from a
1850s shawl.

APPENDIX

KNOWN SHAWL MANUFACTURERS

NAME	LOCATION	DATE	INFORMATION
Allen & Company	Elm Hill	1883	
Baker Roger	Peacock Street	1810	
Barclay William	5 White Lion Street	1801	
Barlow John	Westwick Street	1803	Signatory as Master Weaver to the Wages Agreement
		1816	Died
Barlow Richard Jeremiah	St. Margaret's Parish	1836	
		1841	
		1867	Died on 3rd October aged 72 and is buried at the Rosary Cemetery (Grave Ref: C/347)
Barrow Edward	20 Colegate	1744	born in Manchester
		1783	carrying on business in Norwich as a Yarn Factor
		1784/5	succeeded in making a figured scarf in imitation of the Indian, but did not find a sale for it so manufactured was discontinued.(1840 Mrs. Bardwell in 'A Companion to the Norwich Polytechnic Exhibition')
		1813	Died when living in the parish of St. Saviour, Norwich aged 69.
Basey Charles		1810	
Bidwell & Jarrold		1795	**Agreement** Richard Bidwell, weaver of Norwich and John Jarrold, draper of Woodbridge, Suffolk agree to enter into co-partnership in the Shawl, Scarf and Waistcoat Shape Trade.
		1811 15th May	Notice is hereby given that the Partnership lately subsisting between Richard Bidwell of the City of Norwich and John Jarrold of Dallinghoo in the County of Suffolk carried on at the City of Norwich under the firm of Bidwell & Co., Sack Manufacturers, was this day dissolved by mutual consent and the said trade will in future be carried on by the said Richard Bidwell only, As witness our hands this 15th day of May 1811. Richard Bidwell John Jarrold.
Blake James		1810	
Blake Robert	Heigham	1822	
Blakely Edward	15 Cockey Lane (now known as London Street)	1820	**Advertisements** Edward Blakely respectfully informs his friends and the public that having engaged the shop at present occupied by Miss Theobald he intends opening it by the first week of April. A new and fashionable assortment of Linen, Drapery, Mercery etc.....15 Cockey Lane.
		1820	**Married** Elizabeth Theobald at St. Peter Mancroft **Advertisement** He begs most respectfully to solicit the
	7 Conduit St., Regent Street,		attention of the Nobility, Gentry and the Public to his collection of Silks, Cashmere

KNOWN SHAWL MANUFACTURERS

NAME	LOCATION	DATE	INFORMATION
	London.	1821 17th March	Shawls, Scarfs of Norwich Manufacture. **Advertisements** He announces he had purchased a Linen Drapery and Silk Goods business in London.

		1823
		October
		1824
		1831
			Was selling Norwich, Edinburgh and other shawls and 'a large lot of 8/4 cloth shawls at 5/-d. each'.
			His Billhead
			Edward Blakely, 15 London Lane, Norwich
			       Linen Draper, Silk Mercer etc., Shawl
			            Manufacturer
			        Crapes and Bombazines
			          Funerals Furnished
			Advertisement

		1833 25th August	Her most gracious Majesty, the Queen, and H.R.H. the Duke of Sussex having condescended to patronise the manufacture of Norwich shawls, Edward Blakely begs for inspection on Tuesday
		1840 15th January	15th inst. a splendid assortment of the same description of shawls which Her Majesty has been pleased to select. **Announcement**
		1849 4th August	The Duke and Duchess of St. Albans buy from Edward Blakely several shawls by Shickle, Towler and Campin, one of which was a new pattern of 'a most elegant description'. **Advertisement**
		1849	Gentlemens' plain and embroidered throat ties, travelling shawls and cravats, particularly those of Norwich manufacture **Announcement** Edward Blakely has the honour to inform the Agricultural Gentlemen of the Eastern Counties that he has manufactured and printed some shawls entirely of Norfolk wool, the growth of John Hudson, Esq., of Castleacre. **Society for the Encouragement of the Arts Exhibition of Recent British Manufacturers** Norwich made shawls exhibited by Edward Blakely
	Shawl Manufactory and Print Works, The River House, Duke's Palace.	1850	Llama scarf shawl, yellow ground and a printed ornamental border Silk fillover scarf shawl, blue ground with richly ornamented border Cashmere fillover scarf shawl, Llama scarf shawl, Damask silk scarf shawl. Llama scarf shawl, white ground with printed ornamented borders. Sillk damask scarf shawl (*This shawl was a*

KNOWN SHAWL MANUFACTURERS

NAME	LOCATION	DATE	INFORMATION
	Cheap Warehouse, 6 St. Stephen's Street.	1851	*facsimile of one cut from the loom and presented to Miss Jenny Lind on her visit to Norwich).* Llama scarf shawl, black ground and printed ornamental border. Edward Blakely was awarded a Silver Medal for his shawl fabrics. **Advertisements** Invites attention to his silk grenadine shawls, printed in natural flowers, being the most fashionable styles of the present season.
		1852	**Society for the Encouragement of the Arts Exhibition** Norwich made shawls exhibited by Edward Blakely.
		1853 12th March	Specimen of Norwich shawl weaving, being the first attempt to produce an increased effect by the introduction of gold thread in the shuttle. **The Great Exhibition**
		1851 14th and 21st May	Messrs. Blakely – Cashmere green scarf shawl with gold introduced, shawls of cashmere wool, designed by John Funnell, Anglo-Indian scarfs, shawls, dresses, brocades, etc. Messrs. Blakely were honoured by receiving from Her Majesty two orders for their beautiful shawls made in the pure Indian style. They received a medal for 'a collection of shawls and also for barege scarfs of a novel taste'.
		Queen Street	Appoints R.G. Holmes at Blakely's Cheap Warehouse to sell shawls etc.
		1853 2nd September	**Announcement** Due to alterations to premises a sale of last years goods including woven and printed shawls.
		1854 21st January	**Bankruptcy Announcement** London Street premises bought by N.H. Caley
		1855 12th May	Stock bought by G.L. Coleman and W.P. Edwards Value of Stock £7,862 Conduit Street, London stock bought by
		1855 9th October	Atkinson and Co., of Lambeth, Surrey Value of stock £986. 2. 2
		1856	St. Stephen's Warehouse stock bought by W.P. Edwards. Value of stock £448.10.3 **Starts new business in Queen Street, Norwich.**

KNOWN SHAWL MANUFACTURERS

NAME	LOCATION	DATE	INFORMATION
			January Sale Announcement
			Half-yearly Stocktaking Sale
			Rich selection of British and Foreign
			Manufactures
			The Cashmere Shawl, The Gold Shawl and
			Headed Alhambra Shawls......
			Announcement
			A New Shawl Room will be opened, due to
			increased demand for shawls.
			Advertising shawls of Lyon manufacture.
			Billhead
			Bought of E. Blakely, Queen Street,
			Norwich
			Silk Mercer, Shawlman & Furrier to
			Her Late Majesty, the Queen Dowager
			Funerals completely furnished on the most
			moderate terms
			Terms: Accounts delivered quarterly,
			2 ½ discount allowed.
Blyth Job	St. Paul's	1797 21st September	Received a loan of £25 for three years from the Thomas Doughty Fund for setting up in business as a shawl maker.
		1808	The Mayor's Court ordered that he receive a donation from Sir Thomas White's Fund.
Bolingbroke Charles and Fred and Jones	Church Alley, St. Clement's	1850	
Bolingbroke, Enfield & Co.	Church Alley, St. Clement's	1830 1839	
Breeze Philip	Press Buildings, St. Clement's	1851	
Brown Peter	St. Mary Coslany	1822	
Brown William	St. Clement's	1830	
		1851	Retired and living in the Great Hospital.
Bullimore, Hawkins & Davy	Quayside	1826 15th April	The partnership lately subsisting between William Mark Bullimore, John Charles Hawkins and William Davy carrying on trade in the City of Norwich as Shawl, Bombazine and Crape Manufacturers under the name of Bullimore, Hawkins and Company was dissolved by mutual consent.
Campling John	St. Benedict's	1830	
	Cowgate St.	1836	
Clabburn Thomas	St. Paul's		Thomas, the son of Thomas and Sarah Clabburn (late Houghton) was baptised at St. Paul's Church.
		1830	Living in Magdalen Street and known as a Shawl Manufacturer.
		1847	Had moved to Pitt Street, St. Augustines, with his wife Elizabeth, son Thomas and daughters Amelia and Elizabeth.
		1858	Died aged 70 years and was buried in the

KNOWN SHAWL MANUFACTURERS

NAME	LOCATION	DATE	INFORMATION
			churchyard of St. Augustine's Church. Inside the church is a tablet erected to his memory by upwards of six hundred Weavers of Norwich and Assistants in his establishment as a mark of esteem for his many virtues as an employer and a Good Kind Man.
Clabburn William			Son of Thomas, became partner in the family business from 1846, later principal. One of the founders of the Norwich Crape Company and Chairman of the Company 1876-1888
Clabburn, Plummer & Shaw	Colegate	1839-1844	
Clabburn & Plummer	Pitt Street	1844-1850	
		1844	Registered nine printed shawl designs and nine woven shawl designs at Public Record Office.
		1845	Thomas Clabburn and Charles Taylor Plummer registered two woven shawl designs.
		1846	Registered ten woven shawl designs.
Clabburn, Son & Plummer	Pitt Street	1846	
		1847	Registered three woven shawl designs
		1848	Registered six woven shawl designs
			Registered one woven shawl design
Clabburn, Son & Crisp	Pitt Street	1851-1883	
		1851	**The Great Exhibition** Showed registered figured cashmere shawls, spun silk, fancy silk and Albanian Shawls. Her Majesty The Queen purchased one of their cashmere and silk shawls. H.R.H. Prince Albert purchased one of their 'justly admired and richly executed Hunting Wrappers'
		1854	**Patent No. 1750 – W.H. Clabburn** Improvements in the Manufacture of Shawls and Scarfs. Registered two woven shawl designs.
		1855	Gained first class medal for a reversible shawl. Seventy weavers worked for this firm.
		1858	Registered five woven shawl designs.
		1862	Awarded gold medal at International Exhibition London for silk shawls of superior quality and design. Awarded medal for fillover long shawls made on a Jacquard loom at the Paris Exhibition.
		1863	Made three shawls for presentation by the City of Norwich to Princess Alexandra of Denmark on her marriage to Edward, Prince of Wales. Registered one woven shawl design
		1864	Registered two woven shawl designs.
		1865	Registered four woven shawl designs.
		1872	Registered four woven shawl designs.
		1877	Noted as manufacturing shawls
		1883	Noted as manufacturing shawls

KNOWN SHAWL MANUFACTURERS

NAME	LOCATION	DATE	INFORMATION
Clarke John	St. Paul's	1836	Shawl Manufacturer and Printer
		1852	Died
Cundall & Kerr	The Walk, Market Place	1846	**Itemised bill to Mrs. Fulcher of Bracondale,** Norwich – Norwich Shawl £7
		1865	**Announcement** Cundall and Kerr, now to be known as R. Cundall and Company, 19 Market Place, Norwich. Mantle and Shawl Department Advertisement Offering 'The New Patent Reversible Shawl in great variety…….
Davy Samuel		1851	
Dingle John	38 Botolph Street	1801	
Eastwood William	White Lion Street	1825	**Advertisement** ……selling elegant Silk Shawls, Turnover Handkerchiefs, Shawl Borders and Scarf Ends. Shawls new bordered, fringed and cleaned to look like new. **Announcement** William Eastwood is leaving Norwich for London and is selling off for half price 2,000 silk shawls from 6/6d. to 73/6d. and 10,000 sets of shawl borders and fringes.
Etheridge Phillip Buxton	St. Swithin's	1822	
		1826	**Bankruptcy Announcement**
Etheridge Phillip & Company	St. Martin at Place	1839	Complains of piracies of Scottish Manufacturers – Hand Loom Weaver's Report 1839/40
		1842	
		1851	Retired from business.
Field Frederick	8 Smith's Buildings, City Rd	1851	
Fish John	Fishergate	1801-1811	
Francis John	Calvert Street	1809	Received a loan from the Thomas Doughty Fund.
		1823	Patented a silk/worsted cloth – Patent No. 4776
		1845	Employing 180 persons, 107 female. The women could earn 6/-d. weekly.
		1851	Living in Calvert Street aged 81.
Geary & Sultzer	St. Augustine's	1845	Manufactured shawls, stockings and gloves. Employed a workforce of 600.
		1846	Registered three shawl designs at P.R.O.
Gibbs H. H.	Market Place	1818	**Advertisement** H. Gibbs, Family Linen Warehouse, Shawl Manufacturer, Importer of Irish Tabinets.
Gowen Thomas Love	Church Alley, St. Mary Coslany	1839	
Graves Jeremiah & Son	St. George Colegate	1822	
Grout Bayliss & Company	Patteson's Yard, Magdalen Street	1807	Founded by Joseph Grout, George Grout and John Bayliss
		1815	Moved to New Mills, Norwich
		c1828	Moved to larger premises in Heigham Street
Gunton Thomas & Henry	Pitt Street	1836	Made haircloth as well as shawls.
Herring John & Sons	Gildengate	1806	Exhibited two shawls at the Holkham Shearing from the fleece of Mr. Coke's Southdown sheep.

KNOWN SHAWL MANUFACTURERS

NAME	LOCATION	DATE	INFORMATION
		1807	Mr. Herring Jnr. stated that 117 shawls had that year been made from 224 lbs. of like fleece. – *Norfolk Annals.*
		1851	William Herring Snr. aged 67 had retired from business.
Higgins Christopher	18 Coslany Street Botolph Street	1801	Shawl Manufacturer
		1811	Cotton Manufacturer
		1830	**Bankruptcy Announcement** Christopher Higgins, Shawl Maker, Draper, Chapman, bankrupt. He traded by the buying of silk and manufacturing the same into shawls and selling the same as others of the same trade are used to do.
Higgins Robert		1826	Declared bankrupt and stock sold.
Higgins & Clarke	Pitt Street	1810	
Hinde			
Keymer & Baker	22 Magdalen Street	1801	
King Henry	St. George's Middle Street	1836	
Knights Nicholas	Bishopgate	1801	
Knight P. J.	2 Colegate & 11 King Street, Cheapside, London.	1792	
Laddel William & Co.	Calvert Street	1836	
Mallett Nicholas	5 Muspole Street	1791	**Advertisement**
Massey Thomas	10 Snailgate	1801	Wanted a man who is perfectly acquainted with
		1822	the weaving department of the Fillover Trade, a
		19th May	cottage will be provided for him......
Massey Thomas & Son	Pitt Street	1836	
Metcalfe William	20 Colegate	1799	
Middleton & Answorth	Calvert Street & 16 Waling Street London	1851	
Middleton George	Calvert Street	1850	
Middleton Matthew	Colegate	1810	
		1818	Died
Montieth George			Shawl Warehouse
Oxley John	Market Place	1817	Shawl Warehouse
Paul Thomas	30 Pitt Street	1783	Workrooms
Roberts William	Pottergate	1810	
		1844	Died aged 77, buried at the Rosary Cemetery Ref: E 3/774
Saint Christmas	St. Mary Coslany	1811	Bankrupt
		1854	Died aged 74, buried at the Rosary Cemetery Ref: C 2/389
Sexton Joseph	46 Snailgate	1801	
Shaw & Crisp	Colegate	1845	
		1846	Registered one woven shawl design at P.R.O.
		1848	Registered one shawl design at P.R.O.
Shaw Richard	Colegate	1836	Shawl pattern book in use in 1830s.
Shickle, Towler & Campin	Elm Hill & 48 St. Paul's Churchyard, London	1830 1836	
Sinclair John	Golden Dog Lane	1819	Abstract of Patent No. 4411

KNOWN SHAWL MANUFACTURERS

NAME	LOCATION	DATE	INFORMATION
		1821	Manufacture of shawls and other articles in which coloured threads are wrought into flowers and other fancy figures in weaving......... **Announcement** John Sinclair is leaving the City for 22 Iron-monger Lane, Cheapside, where he intends carrying on bombazine and shawl trade on his own account. He will act as Agent for any Norwich Manufacturer.
Smith, Amiss & Co.		1820	
Smith Robert	Tubby's Yard, Muspole St	1836	At the time of the census he was living in St. Helen's Hospital.
		1851	
Taylor William		1795	**Bankrupt**
Thompson John	Snailgate	1805	
Torris & Sons	The Walk	1842	
Towler, Campin, Shickle &	Elm Hill	1842	
Matthews	Elm Hill	1862	Exhibition – honourable mention for shawls
Towler & Allen	Elm Hill	1872	
Turner Charles	Pottergate	1839	
Vincent James	St. Clement's	1810	
		1822	
Warren & Bateman	Calvert Street	1842	
		1844	Registered four woven shawl designs at P.R.O.
White William	13 King Street	1877	
		1883	
William White & Charles Wright	35 London Lane	1792 1st Nov.	Advertisement ...being connected in the manufacture of Norwich Shawls have always ready for the inspection of the public a large and general assortment of every article in that branch, of the richest patterns and very best fabric, viz: Shawl Cravats, Sashes, Waistcoat Shapes, 6/4 square shawls, ¾ and 4/4 scarves and gown pieces in great variety.
Willement Martin	Bishopgate	1783	
		1794 1st August	**Advertisement** Mr. Willement, having during the last three months been preparing an assortment of shawls, wrought by choice needlewomen, consisting of long and square shawls, waistcoat shapes and riding cravats...on Thursday, 1st August he intends opening his warehouse for the sale of these articles.
Willement Martin & Sons	Colegate	1822	Martin Willement died 8th April 1822
Willement Richard & George	Calvert Street	1822	
Willement Richard	Calvert Street	1842	
		1850	
		1863	
Henry & Edward Willett & Co.	Pottergate	1843	Registered one design at the P.R.O
Edward Willett, Nephew & Co.	Pottergate & 63 Friday Street, London	1850 1872 1879	This old established business ceased trading in 1904
Woodbine John	St. Michael at Thorn	1811	